John Thompson's Modern Course
for the Piano

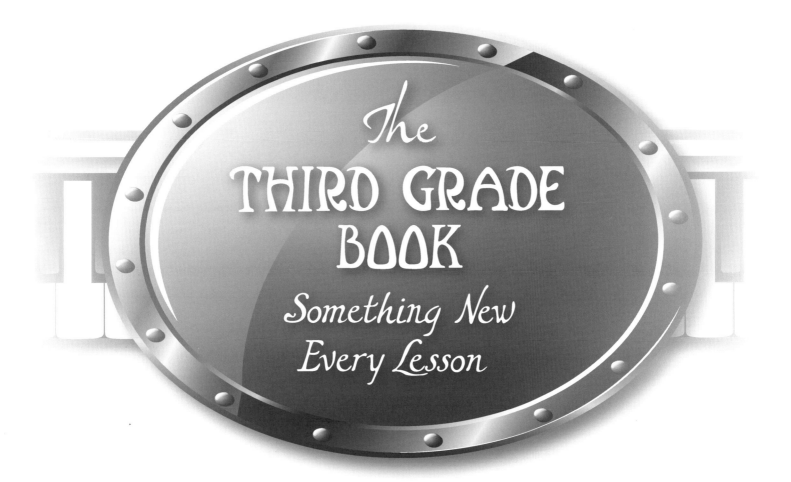

The
THIRD GRADE BOOK
Something New
Every Lesson

Stories and Biographical Sketches by Laurence B. Ellert

**Based on the fundamentals of interpretation; form, mood and style.
Carries on without interruption the musicianship
developed in the 'Second Grade Book'.**

WILLIS MUSIC

THE WILLIS MUSIC COMPANY

PREFACE

This book has been carefully planned to continue the pianistic and musical development of the student from the precise point attained at the end of *The Second Grade Book*. While technical expansion in all directions has been considered and provided for, the main objective of the book is to develop a comprehensive understanding of the basic laws of interpretation.

TEACHING INTERPRETATION

It need scarcely be pointed out that there is a vast difference between imitation and interpretation. Like education itself, interpretation must come from within. We cannot think *for* students, nor can we communicate to them the colour of our own emotional response to music. We can, however, show them where to look in order to determine what any given composer had in mind, and thus lead them to form their own emotional responses, and to intelligently communicate them to the keyboard. The elements of interpretation are therefore presented simply and clearly quite early in the book. Additional helpful notes accompany each example and the student will naturally elaborate on these aids, just so far as his or her ability allows.

VARIETY OF MATERIAL

A single glance at the contents will show that this book covers a wide field in the choice of material. Experience has proven that differences in taste among students are more pronounced at the Third Grade stage of development than in the earlier grades. The teacher may therefore prefer to exercise a certain selectivity in the matter of lesson assignments. There is probably more material in this book than will be needed by an average student. Each example – be it 'La Cucaracha' or the Beethoven 'Septet' – has been thoughtfully and carefully arranged to develop a particular point pianistically and musically speaking.

24 PRELUDES IN ALL KEYS

To assure familiarity with all keys and facility in playing in any or all of them, 24 short preludes are provided on pages 85 to 90 of this book. These preludes are to be assigned throughout the progress of the book as preparatory exercises, in lieu of the usual finger drills.

THE THIRD GRADE VELOCITY STUDIES

Since technical problems become more and more an individual matter as students progress, it has been thought best to handle this phase of the work separately. The author has therefore compiled, edited and annotated a supplementary book entitled *John Thompson's Third Grade Velocity Studies*. It consists of carefully selected and the most effective examples from such master étude writers as Berens, Bertini, Burgmüller, Czerny, Duvernoy, Heller, Kullak, Köhler, LeCouppey, Löschhorn, etc. This little volume makes possible an attractive selection of examples for the development of all phases of pianism and has the advantage of presenting varied styles of technical procedure.

The use of the two books in combination assures a well-rounded musical and technical development for any piano student, young or old. That they may bring distinct pleasure and diversion as well as marked progress to all who use them is the sincere wish of the author.

John Thompson

P.S. Certificate of Merit (Diploma) will be found on page 91.

CONTENTS
'Something New Every Lesson'

CLASSIFICATIONS

Countries represented in folk tune or dance rhythm: America, Cuba, UK,
France, Germany, Hungary, Ireland, Italy, Norway, Poland, Russia, Spain.

ORCHESTRAL MUSIC

Andante from 6th Symphony – Tchaikovsky.

CLASSIC COMPOSERS

J. S. Bach, Beethoven, Bizet, Boccherini, Chopin, Clementi, Grieg, Handel, Humperdinck,
Liszt, Massenet, Rimsky-Korsakov, Rubinstein, Schubert, Schumann, Tchaikovsky.

OPERAS

Jocelyn, *Hänsel and Gretel*, *Carmen*, *Golden Cockerel* and *H.M.S. Pinafore.*

CHAMBER MUSIC

String Quartet – Boccherini; Septet – Beethoven.

LIGHTER CLASSIC

Behr, Burgmüller, Ellmenreich, Godard, Heller, Kölling, Kullak, Popper, Seymour Smith, Sullivan, Waldteufel.

RHYTHMIC FORMS

Ballade, Berceuse, English Dance, Gavotte, Hungarian Dance, March, Minuet, Musette, Romance,
Round, Russian Dance, Sarabande, Serenade, Spanish Dance, Tarantella, Waltz, Witches' Dance.

CROSS-HAND PLAYING

Cross-hand playing is a device used frequently in piano playing. It not only simplifies the perfomance of certain passages, but changes the tonal effect as well. Concert artists sometimes deliberately divide a passage between the hands just to obtain a certain colour and style.

While the following example affords practice in cross-hand work, it should be considered also as a study in tone. Try to develop the best possible singing quality while playing this beautiful spiritual, thus preparing the way for the many examples in lyric form to be found in this book. Remember that tone quality is a part of interpretation.

NOBODY KNOWS THE TROUBLE I'VE SEEN

Track No. 1
Spiritual
Arr. by J. T.

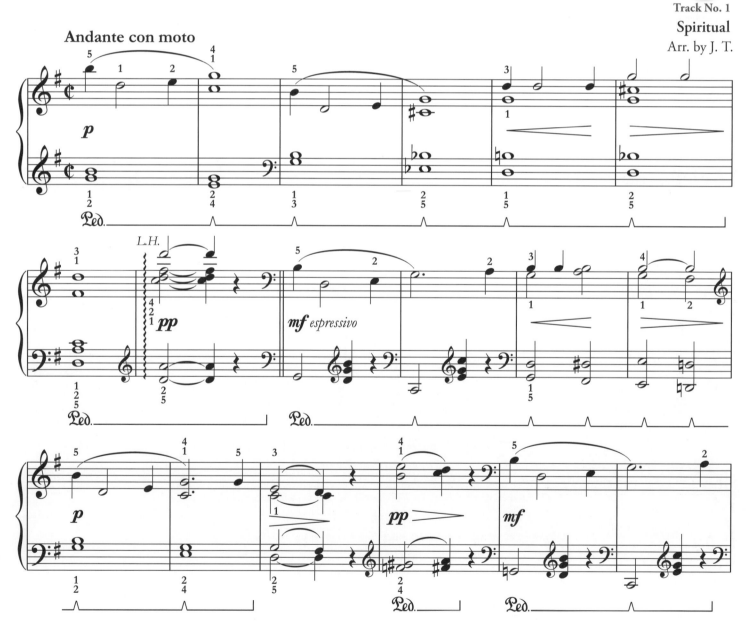

John Thompson's Third Grade Velocity Studies, a compilation of choice études from the master étude composers, has been specially designed to supplement this book.

Teacher's Note: The following chapter on Interpretation should be explained to the student and assigned for careful study at home while this piece is being learned.

INTERPRETATION

There are two sides to music – the material and the emotional.

Playing the notes correctly as indicated on the printed page is but the material side. Translating the feelings and thoughts generated by playing these notes in a certain manner constitutes the emotional side of music and is known as interpretation. The most subtle and complex phase of music study is that of interpretation. Naturally it takes time for this knowledge and skill to develop, and requires some training in the analysis of music.

LAWS OF INTERPRETATION

There are, however, certain fundamental laws of interpretation which should be considered as early as possible in the student's career since they bear directly upon depth of appreciation and understanding as the student progresses. Three key points for the young musician to analyse are form, mood and style.

FORM

Try to discover first of all the form of the composition that you are studying. If, for example, it is in a dance form, it is obvious that rhythm is most important. It is the rhythm that makes the dance. Therefore you should preserve a sharp rhythm and carefully observe all accents. In dance forms it is also obvious that tempo is important. The tempo is indicated by the character of the dance (Minuet, Waltz, Mazurka, etc.), and in modern editions is usually shown by the metronome mark. Set the proper tempo and hold it rather strictly throughout.

Suppose, however, the piece is written in lyric, or song form. In this case interpretation will be quite different. Here, quality of tone is of vital importance. The melody line must be traced and kept intact. Remember the rule, set forth earlier in this course: 'A melody line is always changing in thickness' – and strive for gradation and variety of tone. The rhythm in a lyric piece is more elastic than in the dance form and a certain 'bending' of the tempo, if used sensitively, is desirable.

MOOD

The mood of a composition is determined quite often by the title – otherwise by the character of the music itself. Decide whether the piece is in a happy or sad mood. Also, the depth of the emotional content is to be considered. For instance, is the music humorous or simply cheerful and bright? Is it tragic or merely pensive and reflective? Expression marks offer a certain definite amount of help and, for a time, the young pupil depends upon the guidance of the teacher in these matters. But the sooner he or she is trained to use his or her own powers of analysis, the better. It need hardly be pointed out that the mood of any composition is likely to change with the entrance of a new theme – sometimes even with the entrance of a new phrase – and frequently jumps from one extreme to another.

STYLE

The matter of style is very subtle and difficult to teach. Each composer has an individual style, as has each period of music – Classical, Romantic or Modern. A certain phrase in Beethoven's day, for example, would be given quite different treatment than it would if encountered in a composition by Debussy or more modern composers. For the most part, a knowledge and mastery of style come only after years of study, analysis and intelligent listening and observation. In addition to the above, remember that contrast is a primary law of all art, and search diligently to apply contrast intelligently to each new composition. *Legato* followed by *staccato*; *forte* by *piano*; major by minor; fast by slow – all these devices secure contrast and students should be taught early to consider them as vital factors in interpretation. Naturally it is the fervent hope of the author that all students using this book may develop into young artists, and to do so, they will need to learn the values of good interpretation.

SCHUMANN

Robert Schumann was born on June 8, 1810 in the village of Zwickau, at that time in the Kingdom of Saxony. His father was a book-seller and through that influence young Robert was brought into contact with literature and languages. He was sent to the University of Leipzig to study law. He displayed a gift for music at an early age, and while at the University took up the study of the piano with Friedrich Wieck. He became so interested that he gave up law and devoted himself entirely to music. He fell in love with Wieck's daughter Clara, a fine musician and celebrated pianist, who became his wife in 1840.

In the following year he composed nearly 150 songs, many of which were set to the verses of the German poet Heine. In addition to composing and conducting, he became famous as an editor of a musical magazine. He lived during the Romantic period of the 19th century and is known as a romantic composer.

INTERPRETATION

FORM: This piece is obviously in the Lyric or Song form. Play the right-hand melody with your best possible singing tone while the left-hand accompaniment supplies a subdued, but ever-moving background.

MOOD: It should be played in thoughtful, reflective mood. Not too serious and not too carefree. Keep a moderate tempo and follow the marks of expression.

MELODY

Track No. 2
Robert Schumann
(1810–1856)

MUSETTE

A Musette is an instrument with pipes or reeds and drone in which the wind is supplied by bellows, like a bagpipe. It was modelled on the Irish uilleann, or elbow pipes. The term also applies to a small and primitive kind of oboe.

A royal piper, named Destouches, completely captivated the French Court with his expert performance on the Musette. He had a beautiful instrument covered with velvet and handsomely embroidered with fleur-de-lis; the chanters and drones were of exquisite workmanship.

During the reign of Louis XIV this instrument was exceedingly popular at all royal courts and at the musical entertainments of the nobility. In 1670 it was introduced in the French orchestra. Jean-Baptiste de Lully, a member of the King's famous 'Band of twenty-four', made use of the Musette in the many ballets he wrote for the court. Louis XIV himself danced enthusiastically in these ballets.

Johann Sebastian Bach introduced the Musette form in his English Suites, Nos. 3 and 6; a compliment indeed to the bagpipe and its appropriateness for pastoral dances. The Musette form was also used by Gluck and Handel.

INTERPRETATION

FORM: Dance form. The term Musette applies to both the instrument and the dance that it would accompany. A Musette dance is usually an air in $\frac{2}{4}$, $\frac{3}{4}$ or $\frac{6}{8}$ time, moderate in tempo and suited to the character and range of the instrument. In the following example the broken octaves of the left hand supply the drone effect of the bagpipe against the melodic passages of the right hand.

MOOD: Giocoso, which means sportive, playful. Secure contrast by making wide distinction between piano and forte. Phrase carefully.

MUSETTE

Track No. 3

Johann Sebastian Bach (1685–1750)

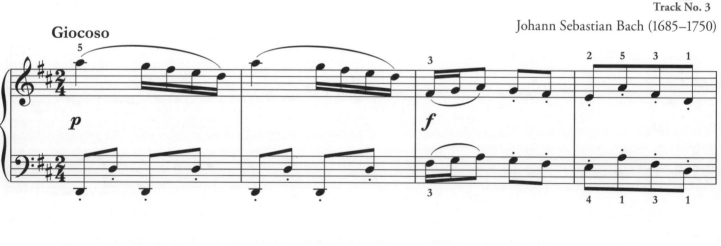

THE MARCH

The March is undoubtedly of military origin. Its dominant characteristic is its vigorous and effective rhythm. During the Middle Ages, the French folk-songs of the period show the influence of the marching Crusaders. A Crusaders' song, bearing the title 'Malbrouch to War has Gone', was used by Napoleon's troops and also by Beethoven in his 'Battle Symphony'. This song bears a strikingly close resemblance to the popular 'For He's a Jolly Good Fellow'.

The refrain of the popular aria for baritone, the 'Toreador Song' from Georges Bizet's Spanish opera *Carmen*, is a colourful example of march rhythm.

In the second act, at the inn of Lillas Pastia, gypsy smugglers, with some officers and soldiers, have been carousing until late into the night. Carmen has been singing and dancing. It is about time to close up for the night. Suddenly, from outside come the sounds of a procession and shouts, 'Hail! Escamillo! Escamillo, the bull-fighter, the champion of the ring at Granada!' Escamillo enters and joins in their toast. Emboldened by the welcome, he assumes an attitude of careless bravado and boastfully sings of the dangers, quick action and triumphs of a toreador. The brilliant uniform, carefree manner and fame of the handsome bull-fighter fairly fascinate Carmen.

The following example has practically the same characteristics as a military march. Set a good tempo and preserve it throughout. Let the rhythm be sharply marked with plenty of accent. Play with spirit and carefree abandon.

TOREADOR SONG
from the opera *Carmen*

Track No. 4
Georges Bizet (1838–1875)

READING ON THREE STAVES

Many passages for piano solo are scored on three staves, and while at first glance this may seem to complicate matters, it will be found upon examination that it actually simplifies the reading. Everybody wants to play songs, and since they are written on three staves, this piece will afford splendid preliminary practice.

In the following example, note that the left hand crosses over the right and plays all the notes on the upper staff. See how effectively you can play this beautiful old Irish Folk song which is also known as 'Danny Boy'. Give to it your best possible singing touch and try to imitate the tones of a cello. Pedal carefully and follow the marks of expression.

LONDONDERRY AIR

Track No. 5

Irish Folk Song

11

OLD ENGLISH DANCE

Dances are continually undergoing changes. All nations have traditionally distinctive forms of folk-dances. English dances may be traced to several categories, including the Sword Dance, the Morris Dance and the Country Dance. The Morris Dance derives its name from 15th-century Moors called Morisco. The Country Dance differs from the others in that it is danced by men and women in couples. Towards the end of the 16th century it had become so popular at the Court of Queen Elizabeth that the Earl of Worcester, in writing of the merry country dances, said: 'Her Majesty is exceedingly pleased wherewith'.

Since 1650 the term Country Dance has been used to define the national dance of England. Court and social dances evidently originated among the peasantry and evolved from adoptions of some of the dances held at the court-balls of France. In 18th-century England, the ball opened with couples promenading around the room to the music of a March; then Minuets were danced, followed by Gavottes and merry Country Dances.

The following is an excellent example of the old English Dance.
It should be played at a moderate tempo, in well-marked rhythm and with stateliness.

DOROTHY

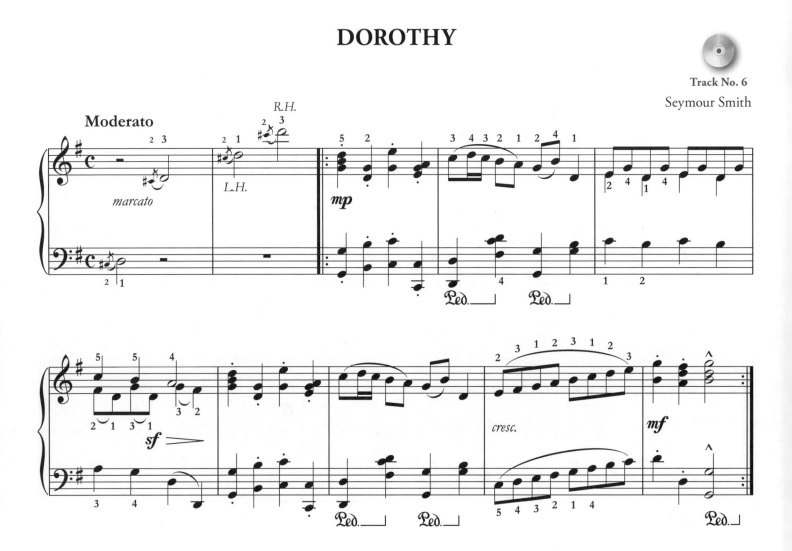

Track No. 6

Seymour Smith

DANCE FORM

The following composition is in the Dance form and rhythm is therefore of paramount importance. Preserve a sharp, brittle rhythm through the entire piece. Set a fairly animated tempo and keep it intact. As suggested by the title, the mood is one of eerie mystery. Make a wide contrast between *legato* and *staccato*. Be sure to give plenty of emphasis to the sudden accents that occur at unexpected intervals. In the last four bars the witches fade away as noiselessly as shadows (*dim. ..... pp*).

WITCHES' DANCE

Op. 4 No. 2

Track No. 7

Theodor Kullak (1818–1882)

SCHUBERT

Franz Peter Schubert, whose lyric compositions are known around the world, was born of very poor parents in Vienna, on January 31, 1797. His father was a school-master and his mother, like Beethoven's mother, had been a cook. When Franz was eight years old his father taught him to play the violin. He had such an exquisite soprano voice at the age of 11 that he was sent to a religious school where boys who sang in the Emperor's Chapel were educated. By the time he was 18 years old he had written 150 songs, and at the age of 31 over 600 songs, many piano pieces, and nine symphonies were credited to his pen.

Schubert lived during a period of great unrest in Europe. Despite his prolific contribution to music he was very poor when he died in Vienna, on November 19, 1828 at the age of 31.

The serenade below was written as a song for mezzo-soprano solo and chorus. Grillparzer, a poet friend of Anna Frölich, wrote the words to celebrate the birthday of one of her students. It was sung for the first time in the open air under moonlight.

SERENADE

Op. 134

Track No. 8

Franz Schubert (1797–1828)

Arr. by J. T.

In piano music, the notation 🎵 indicates that the notes are to be played in a manner long but detached.

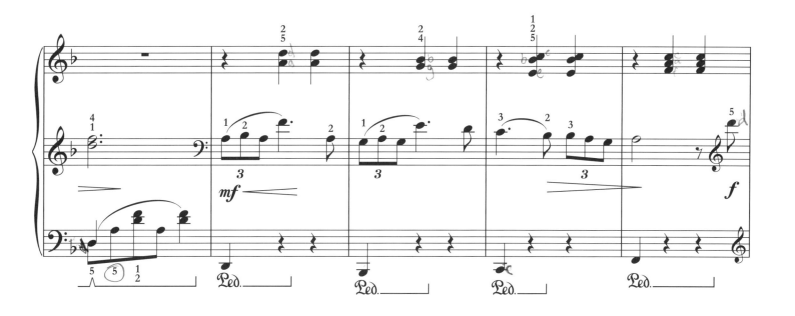

IMITATION

The Spinning Wheel, an English invention of about 1550, was used by early American settlers for spinning their yarn. It was usually made by wheelwrights and consisted of a rotary spindle operated by a flywheel and treadle. The Cherokee people around the Great Smokie Mountains were taught by English colonists to become expert weavers and spinners. A Cherokee wheelwright became quite famous for his beautiful spinning wheels which were frequently presented as gifts to brides and grooms of the grand old mountain-folk.

Descendants of these early colonists still spin as of old. In this photo we depict one of the inhabitants from the 'Heart of the Great Smokies' of Tennessee at her wheel.

The spinning wheel has been the inspiration for many great masters of music; Mendelssohn in his songs, Wagner in his operas, etc. One of the most delightful scenes in Flotow's opera *Martha* is built around the Spinning Wheel Quartet.

The opening notes of the following piece (left hand) depict the starting of the wheel, after which the composer has cleverly injected a constant undercurrent of droning which swells and recedes (*crescendo* and *diminuendo*) as the wheel revolves. Try to hear, mentally, the monotonous song of the spinning wheel which forms the background.

SPINNING SONG

Track No. 9
Albert Ellmenreich
(1816–1905)

GODARD

Benjamin Godard, a romantic composer, was born in Paris on August 18, 1849. During his brief life (46 years) he wrote a series of chamber compositions – trios and string quartets – plus operas and many songs. He orchestrated Schumann's *Scenes from Childhood* which was produced at the Concerts du Châtelet in 1876.

His first opera, *The Jewels of Jeanette* (one act), was given in Paris in 1878. Ten years later, on February 25, 1888, his opera in four acts, *Jocelyn*, was produced in Brussels, and on October 13, it was heard for the first time in Paris. It was only fairly successful, but the 'Berceuse' has won undying popularity. In Act II, outside the cave of the Eagles, Jocelyn (the tenor role), sings the beautiful song which has been here transcribed for piano.

Play this piece quietly in the style of a Cradle song, and make the most of the melody in the second section marked *Andante Moderato*.

BERCEUSE

from *Jocelyn*

Track No. 10

Benjamin Godard (1849–1895)
Transcribed by J. T.

Andante moderato

ACCENTS AND FOREARM STACCATO

> An accent of ordinary intensity.

Accents are also indicated by the sign *sfz* called *sfzorzando*.

The following piece is an étude in forearm staccato.

^ The wedge-shaped accent indicates unusual emphasis.
This should not be confused with the sign, *f* (forte) which means loud.

WILL-O'-THE-WISP

Op. 309 No. 2

Track No. 11

Franz Behr (1837–1898)

CHAMBER MUSIC

The term 'chamber music' commonly applies to instrumental music such as string trios, quartets, etc., suitable for performance in a room or small hall. The early history of chamber music dates back to the 16th century. Giovanni Gabriéli (1557–1612), organist at St Mark's in Venice, experimented with combinations by introducing madrigals for instruments instead of voices. He wrote a canzona for two violins, cornetti, tenor and two trombones which was published in 1615, three years after his death. This was probably the first chamber music.

Chamber music originated in the contacts between musicians and lovers of music. It was written to be played in the drawing rooms of the nobility for the enjoyment of the players and the listeners. In orchestral playing, the effect is the result of a duplication of mass in sound, whereas in chamber music, each player is individual, but the group must think and feel together.

When Louis XIV, 'le grand Monarque', was King of France, he appointed François Couperin his personal music master and the royal organist. Couperin began to develop trios in the concerts he gave every Sunday evening for the King and his court at Versailles. Frederick the Great frequently took part in chamber concerts at Sans-Souci during his reign in Prussia (1740–1786).

In Beethoven's day, chamber music was the popular genre of music played in the home. This great master of the symphony also wrote five string trios, sixteen quartets, two quintets, two sextets, and a septet.

The example on the opposite page is part of a Minuet from his famous Septet in E♭, Op. 70, scored for clarinet in B♭, bassoon, horn in E♭, violin, viola, cello, and bass. He was probably very fond of the opening theme, for he used it (with quite different treatment) in one of his sonatas.

PREPARATORY EXERCISES

For the left hand.

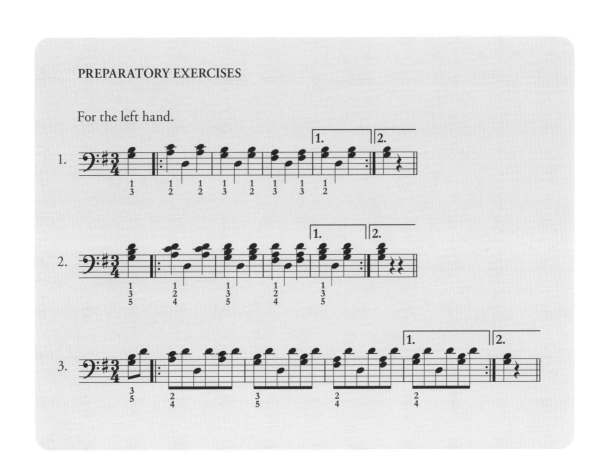

MINUET
from Septet Op. 70

Track No. 12

Ludwig van Beethoven
(1770–1827)

GILBERT AND SULLIVAN

The comic operas of Gilbert and Sullivan have become classic examples of English light opera. Sir Arthur Sullivan was born in London on May 13, 1842. In his youth he sang in a choir. At the age of 25 he wrote a one act operetta, *Cox and Box*, which brought about his partnership with William S. Gilbert and resulted in their many successful entertainments. *Pinafore* was produced in London on May 25, 1878 and for the first time in New York on January 15, 1879. The libretto is a satire on the English navy during the Victorian period. There are two acts. The action takes place on the quarterdeck of 'H.M.S. Pinafore'.

The sailors are scrubbing the deck singing, 'We Sail the Ocean Blue' as Little Buttercup, considerably larger than her name, appears with 'snuff and tobaccy'. All are happy except Ralph Jackstraw who has hopelessly fallen in love with the Captain's daughter, Josephine. She, however, is to be betrothed to the Admiral, Sir John Porter, who has never sailed the sea. Josephine and Ralph plan to elope, but the villain Dick Deadeye overhears the conversation and threatens them.

Sir Joseph tries to win Josephine, believing her shyness is due to his exalted rank; so he explains that love can level all ranks. While Buttercup tries to console the Captain, Deadeye exposes the plot and Ralph is arrested. But Little Buttercup saves the day when she discloses her secret by telling how she nursed two babies many years ago, one of high degree and one of low, and accidently got them mixed; "The well-born baby was Ralph; your Captain was the other." Whereupon the Admiral gives Josephine to Ralph who now takes command of the ship. The erstwhile Captain proposes to Little Buttercup, and the jolly crew sings: "It's greatly to his credit that he's an Englishman."

Excerpts from **H.M.S. PINAFORE**

Track No. 13
Gilbert and Sullivan
(1836–1911) (1842–1900)

THREE CHEERS

give three cheers and one cheer more...

He

is an Eng-lish-man

I'm

Allegretto

called lit - tle   But - ter - cup...

Scherzando

BALLAD

The word 'Ballad' is very old. Coming from the Italian *Ballata*, it means dance with accompaniment. In French, *Ballade* means dancing song. At one time the word 'Ballad' meant a song set to dance rhythm which was danced and sung at the same time. Ballads such as the *Marseillaise* and the *Wacht am Rhein* have had great political influence. Fletcher of Saltoun said: "If a man were permitted to make all the ballads, he need not care who should make the laws of a nation."

In its present form an instrumental ballad is, as a rule, simply an imaginary poem or story set to music. What story or poem does this music suggest to you?

BALLADE

Track No. 14
Friedrich Burgmüller

HANDEL

On February 23rd, 1685 George Frideric Handel was born at Halle, in the eastern part of Germany. He wanted to become a musician but his father insisted that he study law. Nevertheless he learned to play four instruments, and also to compose. By the time he was twelve years old he had become an assistant organist. After his father's death, he devoted his entire time to music, spending three years in Italy and eventually settling in England, where he assumed the post as tutor of the Royal Princesses. He became blind six years before his death in 1759.

The Sarabande, a stately dance of Spanish or Oriental origin, is said to have been invented by a Spanish dancer named Zarabanda sometime about the middle of the 16th century. Its movement is broad and stately, and the metre usually written $\frac{3}{2}$, which means three counts to a bar and one count to each semitone.

This example from Handel is in classic style and the mood, as indicated (Grave), is quite somber. Give all the resonance possible to the broad sweeping chords and try to imitate the sustaining qualities of an organ.

SARABANDE

Track No. 15

George Frideric Handel
(1685–1759)

HUMPERDINCK

Engelbert Humperdinck, German composer, was born in the Rhine province of Siegburg, in September, 1854. One day his sister, Mrs Wette, wrote a series of verses based on Grimm's fairy tale *Hänsel and Gretel* for her children, to be used for a home Christmas celebration. She sent them to her brother to be set to music. The work was so enjoyable that later they expanded it into a full opera in three acts. In writing the score, Humperdinck made frequent use of German folk songs. The first performance in Weimar on December 23, 1893 was an instantaneous success and equally so in New York on October 8, 1895.

Once upon a time, in a cottage by the woods, there lived a poor broom maker, his wife, and two children, Hänsel and Gretel. As they needed food, the father and mother go to sell brooms, leaving the children to do the house work. They soon grow tired and hungry, so Gretel cheers Hänsel with a song, 'Brother, Come Dance with Me'. When their mother returns, she scolds them for neglecting their work and sends them into the woods to pick berries.

By nightfall they have eaten all the berries and are lost in the forest. Tired, they rest under a tree. The Sandman comes, they say their 'Evening Prayer' and fall asleep, while angels descend and watch over them. Awakened by the Dawn Fairy, they are surprised to see a sugar-candy house nearby, the home of the wicked witch of Ilsenstein. She enchants Hänsel, locks him in a cage and dances with glee at the prospect of a meal. Then she seeks Gretel, intending to bake her in the huge oven. But Gretel finds a magic wand and pushes the witch in instead. Lo and behold! The spell is broken, the oven falls apart, the Gingerbread children come to life, their fathers and mothers find them and all dance merrily.

BROTHER, COME DANCE WITH ME

from *Hänsel and Gretel*, Act I

Track No. 16
Humperdinck (1854–1921)
Adapted by J. T.

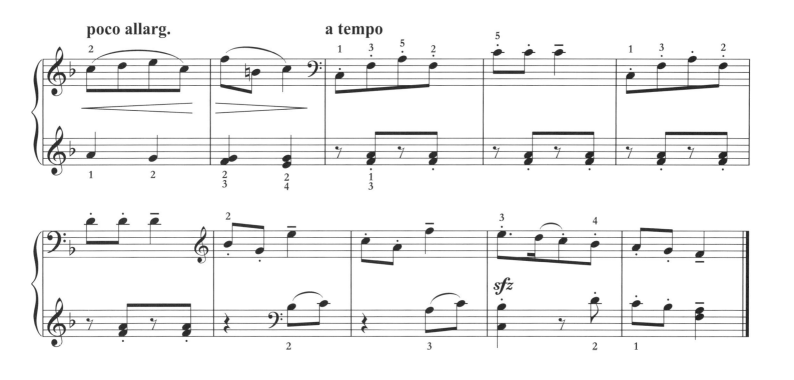

EVENING PRAYER

from *Hänsel and Gretel*, Act II

Track No. 17

Humperdinck (1854–1921)

Adapted by J. T.

J. S. BACH

Piano students owe more to Johann Sebastian Bach than to any other composer of the Baroque period. Before his time, due to the system of tuning, many accidentals sounded out of tune. Bach, who had always tuned his own clavier, used the well-tempered system of tuning which made it possible to play with equal ease in all major and minor keys. Then he composed his famous *Well-Tempered Clavier* (two volumes of Preludes and Fugues written in each major and minor key). He also introduced a systematic use of the thumb – a custom not observed before – which greatly increased the technical possibilites of keyboard instruments.

The word 'Prelude', as its name suggests, is a preliminary movement; a sort of introduction to the main body of a composition. However, the term is often used to designate a short number, complete in itself.

In playing this Prelude from Bach, be sure to observe strictly the marks of phrasing.

The little embellishment found on the third line (left hand) is called a *Mordent*.

Written

Played

Be sure to play the first note of the mordent exactly on the beat, together with the right-hand note.

PRELUDE IN C

Track No. 18
Johann Sebastian Bach (1685–1750)

THE HARPSICHORD

The Harpsichord was an important instrument of the 16th, 17th and early 18th centuries. Instead of being struck by hammers, the strings were plucked by quills set upon wooden jacks. The compass was 4 ½ octaves. The harpsichord and clavichord (*Clavis* being the Latin name for keys and *Chorda* meaning strings) were the forerunners of the piano.

Bartolomeo Cristofori (1655–1731) of Padua, Italy, was renowned as a famous harpsichord maker. When Prince Ferdinand di Medici heard of him in 1716, he appointed him instrument maker in Florence. In this capacity he made the first pianoforte.

During the reign of Louis XIV, Jacques Champion de Chambonières was the foremost representative of harpsichord music. He was the teacher of François Couperin, the Elder (1681–1698), uncle of the celebrated François referred to on page 26.

Early sonatas and sonatinas were composed for the harpsichord and clavichord. As these instruments were small and light and easily carried from one room to another, the tone was correspondingly delicate. Consequently, the limitations of these instruments should be kept in mind when performing such music on a modern piano. Delicacy of tone and grace of style is of utmost importance. In general, avoid robust *fortes* and *bravura*.

Muzio Clementi was born in Rome on January 24, 1752. His father was a goldsmith and amateur musician. At the age of 14 his musical talent was so evident that an English gentleman who heard him play obtained his father's permission to educate him in England. He amassed a fortune from teaching, performing concerts, composing and his success as a manufacturer of pianos.

Sonatina means 'little sonata'. The word 'sonata' literally means 'sound piece'. In the early days an instrumental piece was called *sonata* to distinguish it from a vocal piece, which was called *cantata*. Later, both words assumed a more definite musical meaning, having to do with form.

This perfect example of a 'little sound piece' by Clementi has the character but not the form of a true sonata. It was composed in three movements, but for the present the first movement is quite adequate. It should be played in a classical style.

SONATINA
Op. 36 No. 1

Track No. 19
M. Clementi (1752–1832)

THE ROUND

Singing by groups, referred to as choral singing, originated many centuries ago. In ancient Greek drama, the 'chorus' were spectators of the play who expressed their sentiments in songs between the acts. Musical contests were frequently included in the Olympic games. With the advent and spread of Christianity, part-songs (choral music) began to take form. Soon, however, church music began to evolve towards the style we call polyphonic ('many voiced') music which was sung in three and four parts by the choirs.

The Round is among the early forms of choral music, dating from a period of which there are but few records. It was very popular in England during the 16th and 17th centuries. From 1843 to 1911 there was a Society in London, 'The Round, Catch and Canon Club', founded for the purpose of singing the new compositions in the form of round, catch or canon.

A round is a piece designed in one part but so ingeniously planned that it can be taken up at stated periods, continually passing *'round and 'round* by several voices which combine in pleasing harmony. Most people are familiar with the famous round 'Three Blind Mice'.

'Dona Nobis Pacem' is an old Christmas round written by an unknown German composer of the 16th or 17th century. It is quite widely used in several European countries and is arranged here as a piano solo, but may also be used very effectively as a choral piece.

First: Have the students learn the complete melody in unison. Next, divide the singers into three groups; two groups of sopranos and one of altos. If there are boys, divide into sopranos, altos and a group of boys.

Each group sings through the round three times. However, they begin and end at different times. The first group begins by singing the first line (No. 1). As this group begins the second line (No. 2), the second group begins by singing the first line (No. 1). Two-part singing is now in effect. As the first group reaches the third line (No. 3) and the second group begins the second line (No. 2), the third group begins the first line (No. 1) and from this point three-part choral singing is heard in good harmony until the various groups drop out, one group at a time, as they come to the end of the third rendition.

To my friend Peter Dykema, who brought this beautiful round to my attention.

DONA NOBIS PACEM *(Grant Unto Us Peace)*

Track No. 20

Anon.
Arranged by J. T.

MEXICAN FOLK SONG

'La Cucaracha' (the cockroach) is a Mexican folk song said to have originated in the army. In some countries the lowly cockroach is omnipresent and is joked about. As with all army songs, this one has a countless number of verses – each new regiment doing its bit by way of addition. It has been adapted here in the form of an exercise for passing under the thumb.

Play the repeated notes, divided between the hands, *marcato* – well marked – and let all *staccatos* be crisp and brittle. Observe the sustained notes in the left hand in bars 14 to 20 and be sure to note where the melody lies in the bass part on page 45, lines two and three.

LA CUCARACHA

(The Cockroach)

Track No. 21

Mexican Folk Song

Adapted by J. T.

WALTZ

The Waltz (In German, *Walzer*, French, *Valse*, Italian, *Valzer*) is a round dance in $\frac{3}{4}$ time, varying from slow to moderately fast, first appeared in Bavaria and Austria in about 1780. Its origin has been attributed to Bohemia, Germany and France. When the waltz was introduced in England in 1812, society was quite shocked. In country dances, the participants indulged in nothing more intimate than touching each others' hands; imagine therefore, the sudden effect waltzing couples made, who, almost embracing each other, were swinging about the ballroom with whirling motion.

Émile Waldteufel was born in Strasbourg, Alsace on December 9, 1837. He studied music at the Paris Conservatoire and later was employed in a piano factory. At one time he was appointed Court Pianist to the Empress Eugénie, wife of Napoleon III. He published his first waltzes at his own expense and after considerable success devoted himself exclusively to this type of music.

Establish a good rhythm from the very beginning and preserve it throughout. Play the first theme in a well-sustained manner, and *espressivo*. Phrase off the two-note slurs in the second theme rather sharply. Make sharp contrast between *staccato* and *sostenuto* in the third theme. Be sure to emphasise the counter theme in the last part of the next (trill) section. End with a brilliant Coda.

THE SKATERS
Waltz

Track No. 22
Emil Waldteufel (1837–1915)
Adapted by J. T.

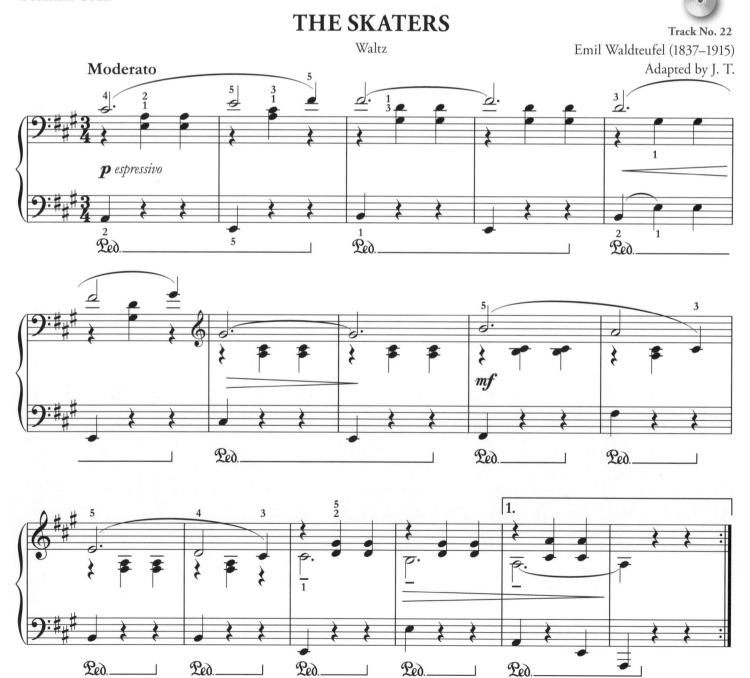

49

GRIEG

Edvard Grieg was born in Bergen, Norway, on June 15, 1843. He received his early musical training from his mother. At the age of 15 he met the idol of his dreams, the noted Norwegian violinist, Ole Bull, who related astounding stories of his journeys to America. This paved the way to direct Grieg's musical career. After graduating from the school in Germany founded by Mendelssohn, he returned to Norway and devoted himself to the cause of national Norwegian music. At his death, in 1907, 57 governments sent official representatives to attend his funeral.

Grieg had his inspiration for the 'Watchman's Song' from a performance of Shakespeare's Macbeth. Written in lyric style, it is a simple song for piano depicting the humming of a Night Watchman.

Do not allow the tempo to drag–the alla breve sign offsets somewhat the *molto andante* in the text. About ♩ = 96 is the correct tempo. The middle section is in the form of a short intermezzo and portrays the Spirit of the Night. This section should be played *misterioso*, beginning very softly and growing into *forte* in the third and fourth bars. The arpeggio passage should be rolled rather than fingered, with fingers kept close to the keys. Like most of Grieg's compositions, this piece calls for vivid imagination on the part of the performer.

WATCHMAN'S SONG
Op. 12 No. 3

As I did stand my watch upon the hill,
I looked toward Birnam, and anon, me thought,
The wood began to move.   *Macbeth.*

Track No. 23
Edvard Grieg
(1843–1907)

Molto andante e semplice

Intermezzo (Spirit of the Night)

ITALIAN DANCE

A Tarantella is an Italian dance which derives its name from the legend originating in Taranto, a city in the mountain country, in the 'heel of the boot' of Italy. This city gave its name to the venomous spider, the tarantula. According to tradition, if anybody bitten by the dreaded spider dances the Tarantella hard enough, and long enough, they will prevent themselves from falling into a coma and eventually yielding to the deadly poison.

The story above gives a definite clue to interpretation. The tempo is quite fast. Learn the piece first by counting six to the bar – one count to each quaver. Then, as speed develops, it should be played two counts to the bar. One count to each dotted crotchet, or group of three quavers. The mood is of ever-increasing excitement, beginning with *Vivace* and becoming more furious. Be sure to observe the frequent two-note slurs, a characteristic of the Tarantella.

TARANTELLA

Track No. 24
John Thompson

52

THE SYMPHONY ORCHESTRA

The symphony orchestra, as we know it today, developed from chamber music and Corelli's 'Band of Twenty-four' in the service of Louis XIV. During his residence at the Esterhazy Palace, Haydn, who had been so successful with his string quartets, began to group his small orchestra into four separate sections: (1) the String section: violins, viola, cello, double bass; (2) the Woodwind section: flute, clarinet, oboe, bassoon; (3) the Brass section: trumpets, French horn, trombone, tuba; (4) the Percussion section: drums, cymbals, bells, gongs. This is the physical form and balance of the famous symphony orchestras which render the masterpieces of Haydn, Mozart, Beethoven, etc. Symphonic music is actually a Sonata for orchestra, a harmonious mingling of sounds bearing witness to the influence of historic events, geographical and political changes. Mozart wrote his great symphonic examples in 1788 but it remained for Beethoven to bring the symphony to its most perfect stage of development.

PYOTR ILYICH TCHAIKOVSKY

Pyotr Ilyich Tchaikovsky was born in Votkinsk, Russia, on May 7, 1840. His father, a government inspector of mines, was a very prominent man in the district. His mother came of a French family which had emigrated to Russia during the Revolution. At the age of four, Pyotr received piano lessons from a governess. When he was eight years old the family moved to Moscow and later to St Petersburg. In 1859 he graduated from the School of Jurisprudence and entered the Ministry of Justice as a clerk. In 1862 he decided to devote himself entirely to music and composing. His String Quartet, Op. 11 was played for the first time at a concert given in honor of Tolstoy in 1876, and in the same year he began the famous correspondence with Nadezhda von Meck. In 1891 he visited the United States and took part in the concerts played for the dedication of Carnegie Hall.

The short excerpt on page 55 is from Tchaikovsky's Symphony No. 6 in B Minor, known as the 'Pathétique'. It is one of the most popular of orchestral works and belongs to the giants of music. The idea came to him as he was setting out on a journey to Paris in December 1892. In writing to Davidov, to whom the work is dedicated, Tchaikovsky said: "During the journey, while composing it in my mind, I often wept bitterly." He conducted the first performance (in St Petersburg, on October 16, 1893) himself and was convinced that it was his greatest work. Nine days later he died. Some have pointed to a fragment of the Russian requiem in the first movement as significant that it was to be his last work.

This andante has a beautifully structured melody and an underlying sense of melancholy. Play the right-hand theme with the pressure touch. Pay strict attention to phrasing and expression marks. Use pedal only as indicated.

ANDANTE FROM 6TH SYMPHONY

Op. 74 'Pathétique'

Track No. 25
Pyotr Tchaikovsky (1840–1893)

COURT DANCE

The Gavotte is an old French court dance form, trod by the courtiers of the 16th and 17th centuries. It is said to have been derived from Gavòt, a dialect spoken in Dauphiné.

For a time the Gavotte was neglected, but it was revived by Marie Antoinette. Her teacher, Christoph Willibald Gluck (1714–1787), famous as the father of French opera, composed special music for her and the dance became quite popular at Versailles. After the Revolution, the Gavotte was once more revived.

The example beginning on this page is an arrangement of a very famous Gavotte written for a cello solo by David Popper, himself a cellist of the first rank. Born in Prague in 1846, he displayed early evidence of remarkable talent, and he made extensive concert tours in Europe.

The Gavotte is in common time of moderately fast movement and always begins on the third beat of the bar. Pay attention to the contrasting *staccato* and *legato*, keep an even tempo and observe the dynamic marks.

GAVOTTE

Track No. 26
David Popper (1846–1913)
Adapted by J. T.

57

THE STRING QUARTET

String quartets are one of the most popular forms of chamber music. There are examples of quartets for stringed instruments as far back as the time of Allegri (1584–1652), a musician of the Papal Chapel in Rome who wrote a four-part sonata for strings. The string quartet as we know it was developed by Haydn (1732–1809), who, as court musician for the Prince of Esterhazy on his Hungarian estates, devoted much of his time to composing chamber music for special occasions. He wrote more than 65 string quartets.

Luigi Boccherini, a contemporary of Haydn, was born in Lucca, Italy, on February 19, 1743. He was a fine cellist and became chamber musician to the Infante Luis of Spain. Most of the music of his day was written for voice in four parts which inspired him to arrange it for four stringed instruments. In 1787 Friederich Wilhelm of Prussia conferred on him the title of chamber composer. Boccherini wrote over 100 string quartets and over 150 string quintets. Scored for first violin, second violin, viola, and cello, each instrument has its own distinctive charm.

MINUET

from String Quartet

Track No. 27
Luigi Boccherini (1743–1805)

ROMANCE

A romance was originally a ballad in verse, but was later transferred to stories of love and tales of knightly chivalry. The term applies more to the character than the actual form of a musical composition. In other words, it is an expression of personal sentiment rather than precise structural form.

The Romantic period of the 19th century was indeed an era of the melodist. Schubert, Mendelssohn, Chopin, Schumann, Rubinstein, Massenet, etc. were active in Europe while Stephen Foster (1826–1864), the father of the American ballad, was inspired at home. Many European musicians started to tour America. When Paderewski passed through a town, hundreds rushed to the railroad station.

RUBINSTEIN

Anton Grigorevich Rubinstein was born in Vichvatinets, Russia, on November 28, 1829. His mother was well-educated in music and literature. When he was five years old she found him taking an interest in sheet music, and immediately began to give him piano lessons. At this time his happy-go-lucky father moved his family to Moscow and established a pencil factory. During the next four years Anton studied under the noted master, Villoing. In 1840, he was taken to Paris where Liszt proclaimed him 'an infant prodigy' and encouraged him to play in other cities. He also played for Chopin, Queen Victoria of England and the Queen of Holland. At one of his concerts, Mendelssohn conducted him to the piano. His fame as the 'Russian boy with fingers as light as a feather' spread to every continent.

After the death of his father, he settled in St Petersburg as a teacher-composer, also giving occasional concerts. In 1849, the grand Duchess Helen made him court pianist. After another concert tour he became the director of a conservatory in St Petersburg but was obliged to give it up in 1867 because of pressing concert engagements. Czar Alexander II decorated him with the Order of Vladimar in 1869.

An enthusiastic reception awaited Rubinstein on his arrival in the U.S. in 1872. He played in 215 concerts. In most of them he played his own compositions, among which the 'Romance' was always a favourite.

ROMANCE

Play with your best possible singing tone and try to give to the interpretation a feeling of deep sentiment and poetic eloquence.

Track No. 28

Anton Rubinstein (1829–1894)
(Adapted by J. T.)

RUSSIAN FOLK SONG

There was a proverb in old Russia: 'Song is truth; and the expression of our life'. Nearly every activity of the daily life of the Russian people was expressed by some lyric to accompany it. Many Russian folk tunes suggest the fiery, vigorous and fascinating rhythms of the Orient, an atmosphere of colour, mystery and vitality. Decisive and intense rhythm is omnipresent in all Russian folklore.

Many of the livliest and most dashing folk-dances, especially music of gypsy origin, are written in the minor mode as we have experienced in playing the Russian Gypsy song 'Two Guitars' in *The Second Grade Book*.

In order to emphasise the syncopation be sure to observe all accents, staccatos and sostenuto marks. Set a lively tempo and pedal only as marked.

BUBLITCHKI

Pretzels

Track No. 29

Russian Folk Song

MASSENET

Jules Massenet, a famous French composer, was born on May 12, 1842. His father had been an officer under Napoleon Bonaparte. His mother, who was very musical, taught him the elements of music by placing his tiny hands on a piano and writing the notes corresponding to the black and white keys with their respective positions on lines and spaces on a strip of paper and stretching it on the piano keyboard.

His progress in music and composition was marvellous. Before he was 21 years old, he won the Grand Prix de Rome with his cantata *David Rizzio*. This prize entitled him to a period of study in Italy. Upon his return to Paris, he entered seriously upon the work of composition. His works consist of operas (*Roi de Lahor, Esclarmonde, Herodiade, Cid, Werther*, etc.), orchestral music, piano music, and songs.

This composition is in lyric form. The mood is wistful and sad. This effect is obtained by the chromatic descent of the left-hand melody. Be sure to observe the passages marked with a curved line and the dots, thus ⌣‥‥. This indicates a passage of long, but detached notes, similar to playing *sostenuto*. Strive for the utmost expression.

MELODY

Track No. 30
Jules Massenet (1842–1912)

LISZT

Franz Liszt composed 15 Hungarian Rhapsodies. The second is perhaps the best known and loved of the entire set. The word *Rhapsodie* pertains to the form of the composition and is used to designate a work fantastic in character, which does not adhere to the more conventional forms, and is built upon more or less isolated fragments.

Gypsy music is characterised by the absence of restraint. It is as free as the wind blows, and is always intensely expressive. Since it is for the most part improvised, it follows closely the varying mood of the performer and is apt to range from deepest melancholy to fiery abandon.

Liszt's Hungarian Rhapsodies were constructed on Gypsy airs. The Gypsies are more respectfully known as the Romani people, an ethnic group thought to have emigrated from India. Many settled in Hungary, where they found a real sympathy toward their music, which was finally adopted as the national music of Hungary.

In composing his rhapsodies Liszt usually chose airs that portrayed contrasting emotions. The 'Lasson', for example, is a slow and mournful song of deepest depression. This is followed by the 'Friska', a bright, playful and capricious dance, and ends with the 'Czardas', furious in character and quite as intoxicating rhythmically as the 'Tarantella' of Italy or the Dervish dances of the Orient.

The three moods can be easily recognised in the following adaptation of the ever popular 'Hungarian Rhapsodie No. 2' by Franz Liszt.

Adaptation of
HUNGARIAN RHAPSODIE NO. 2

Track No. 31

Liszt (1811–1886)
(Adapted by J. T.)

FRISKA

CHOPIN

Frédéric Chopin's compositions reflect joy and sorrow for his beloved Poland. Stanislaus Augustus was the last King of Poland. Under this unfortunate sovereign the country suffered a long and devastating war, besieged by Cossacks and Muscovite soldiers. Then came the division, Catherine II of Russia, Maria Teresa of Austria and Frederick the Great each taking a slice of unhappy Poland. In 1830 a revolution took place but ended in the surrender of Warsaw and the dispersion of the Polish people. In 1832 what remained was declared part of the Russian Empire. Chopin's grief over the loss of Polish independence reached its climax in the 'Funeral March' – the third movement of his Sonata No. 2, Op. 35.

Play this Prelude in a manner that suggests the solemnity of a funeral procession. Try to obtain utmost resonance. Use arm attack and give a little emphasis to the upper, or soprano voice. Apply the pedal immediately after each chord has been struck.

PRELUDE IN C MINOR

Op. 28 No. 20

Track No. 32

Frédéric Chopin (1810–1849)

MINUET

The Minuet, in French, *Menuet*, from *menu* – small (referring to small steps), is one of the earlier dance forms supposed to have originated in the French province of Poitou about the end of the 17th century.

The minuet is in triple time, has a slow, stately movement, and frequently occurs in suites, sonatas and symphonies.

During the 18th century this dance form became the favourite at many of the court balls in Europe. English Christmas parties danced gaily to its graceful rhythm. In colonial America it was especially popular in Virginia.

Beethoven's 'Minuet in G' is an excellent example. While he used the minuet form in many of his works he was the first to introduce in its place, in sonata and symphony, the livelier *scherzo*.

Simplicity is the real charm of this famous Minuet. Play with expression but avoid extremes. The trio section may be played a trifle faster than the first two sections. Observe strictly the pedal and phrasing marks.

MINUET IN G

Track No. 33
Ludwig van Beethoven (1770–1827)

CURIOUS STORY

Track No. 34

Stephen Heller
(1813–1888)

Molto vivace ♩ = 184

PREPARATORY EXERCISES

No. 1

No. 2

No. 3

HYMN TO THE SUN

from the opera *The Golden Cockerel*

Nikolai Rimsky-Korsakov
arr. by J. T.

Moderato ♩ = 100

dim. poco a poco

L.H.

L.H.

L.H.

Ped.

rit.

molto rit.

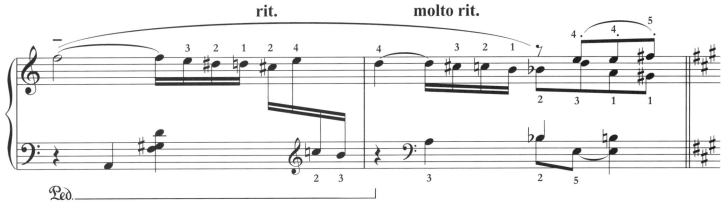

Ped.

24 PRELUDES

The following 24 Preludes in all keys, built upon familiar pianistic patterns,
may be assigned as preparatory studies in place of the usual finger drills.

PRELUDE NO. 1
Cross Hand

Track No. 36

PRELUDE NO. 2
Balloons

Track No. 37

PRELUDE NO. 3
Scherzino

Track No. 38

PRELUDE NO. 4
Spanish Dance

Track No. 39

PRELUDE NO. 5
Whims

Track No. 40

PRELUDE NO. 6
Sparks

Track No. 41

PRELUDE NO. 7
March Wind

Track No. 42

PRELUDE NO. 8
Mystery

Track No. 43

PRELUDE NO. 14
Arabesque

Track No. 49

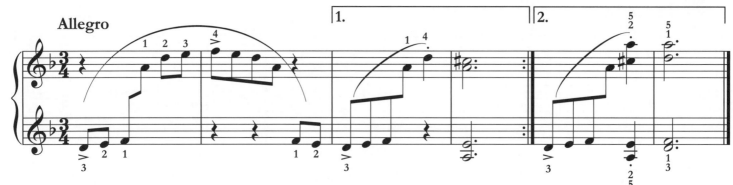

PRELUDE NO. 15
March

Track No. 50

PRELUDE NO. 16
The Fountain

Track No. 51

PRELUDE NO. 17
Scherzino

Track No. 52

PRELUDE NO. 18
Funeral March

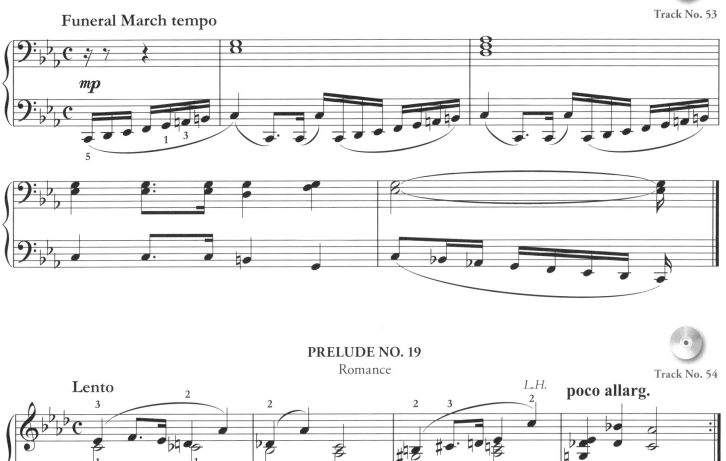

PRELUDE NO. 19
Romance

PRELUDE NO. 20
Arpeggi

PRELUDE NO. 21
In Old Castile

Track No. 56

PRELUDE NO. 22
Lament

Track No. 57

PRELUDE NO. 23
Dance

Track No. 58

PRELUDE NO. 24
Orientale

Track No. 59

Certificate of Merit

This certifies that

. . . .

has successfully completed

John Thompson's Third Grade Book

and is eligible for promotion to

John Thompson's Fourth Grade Book

Teacher . . . .

Date . . . .

JOHN THOMPSON (1889–1963)

Talented American pianist/composer John Thompson was born in Pennsylvania. At an early age he appeared as a concert pianist in all of the principal cities of America and Europe, where his brilliant playing received the highest praise. After concluding his triumphant concert career he headed music departments at conservatories in Philadelphia, Indianapolis and Kansas City. During these tenures he developed certain definite and original ideas about teaching, and in a short time became famous for his sincere efforts to interest young pupils in pianism. All of his books teach, in the simplest language possible, interpretation and expression. One ideal is 'to use in miniature the same attacks as those used by the concert artist.'

© Copyright 1937 The Willis Music Company
Florence, Kentucky, USA. All Rights Reserved.

Exclusive Distributors:
Music Sales Limited
Newmarket Road, Bury St Edmunds, Suffolk IP33 3YB, UK.
Music Sales Pty Limited
Units 3-4, 17 Willfox Street, Condell Park NSW 2200, Australia.

Order No. WMR101112
ISBN: 978-1-84938-886-3

This book © Copyright 2012 The Willis Music Company, Florence, KY, USA.
All Rights Reserved.

Engravings by Paul Ewers Music Design.
Edited by Toby Knowles.
CD mastered by Jonas Persson.

Printed in the EU.

CD TRACK LISTING

Each track is split—hear both piano and accompaniment if the balance is centred,
and the accompaniment only if the balance control is to the left!